traditional **puddings**

Essential dishes for everyday cooking

Notes for the reader
This book uses both metric and imperial measurements. Follow the same units of measurement throughout; do not mix metric with imperial. All spoon measurements are level, unless otherwise stated: teaspoons are assumed to be 5 ml and tablespoons are assumed to be 15 ml. Unless otherwise stated, milk is assumed to be semi-skimmed, eggs and individual vegetables such as potatoes are medium, and pepper is freshly ground black pepper. Recipes using raw or very lightly cooked eggs should be avoided by infants, the elderly, pregnant women, convalescents and anyone suffering from an illness. The times given are an approximate guide only.

Contents

introduction

From fresh fruit creations to sumptuous steamed puddings, home-made sweets range from the classic to the contemporary. Traditional puddings and desserts come in all shapes and sizes and that hint of sweetness provides us all with comfort and enjoyment. Some desserts are so quick and easy to make that there's really no excuse not to indulge!

Puddings have firmly established themselves in today's modern cuisine. Creating delicious desserts is much easier than you may think and can easily become part of your weekly routine, even in the busiest of households. You don't have to spend all day slaving in the kitchen to create a delicious masterpiece. Many special-occasion desserts can be fully prepared in advance, leaving you free to spend time with your family or guests. Choose from your favourite puddings of your childhood or update classic recipes with contemporary flavours.

A Healthy Body

With today's increased focus on healthy eating, it is easy to think that desserts are too much of an indulgence to be included in our everyday diets. However, it is worth remembering that your body's craving for the sweet stuff is something that is down to biochemistry, not just self-indulgence. In the winter months when your body needs more energy to keep warm, the simple sugars in desserts offer a quick boost. It is also said that eating something sweet after a meal helps the body to digest protein and fat properly, ensuring you get maximum energy from your main meal. In addition, fruit-based desserts can make a valuable contribution to our diets, helping us a step further towards achieving that important five-a-day. All in all, there is no reason why traditional puddings cannot be enjoyed as part of a balanced diet and healthy lifestyle.

Traditional Puddings is split into four chapters, making it easy for you to find the recipe you need.

The Usual Suspects

The nostalgia that accompanies proper puddings will never fade away. As traditional desserts enjoy a revival across the country, classic recipes are reappearing on menus of pubs and bistros. Why not try re-creating your favourites at home? Traditional puddings, such as Treacle Tart, Rice Pudding and Steamed Syrup Sponge Pudding, are perfect for a warming winter treat, while Banana Splits will be enjoyed by adults and children alike.

Chocolate Galore

We all love chocolate but its versatility is often forgotten. Family favourites like Chocolate Fudge Cake are always a hit, but have you considered using chocolate in a different way? Surprise your guests with a Chocolate Fondue at a party or gathering, or whip up a batch of dainty Chocolate Éclairs to serve at a coffee morning. And if you don't have time to make a pudding, but desire something sweet, then a warming Real Hot Chocolate can be the perfect solution.

Fruity Favourites

A fruit pie – fresh from the oven and served with a spoonful of cream or custard – is for many of us the epitome of comfort food. For a variation on the pie theme, crumbles, cobblers and clafoutis are infinitely versatile and can be made using whatever fruit is in season for the fullest flavour. And for those with a taste for something a little more contemporary, Tarte au Citron is a modern twist on the classic fruit pie, with added zest!

Cool Classics

No sweet menu is complete without a selection of chilled desserts, many of which can be prepared in advance and chilled in the refrigerator until you are ready to serve. Classic dishes, such as Strawberry Cheesecake, are always in demand and Trifle is perennially popular. For a continental flavour, try the Italian favourite – Tiramisù. Or you could prove that home-made really does taste best by making Rich Vanilla Ice Cream. It is perfect either on its own or served as an accompaniment to a wide range of both hot and cold desserts.

the usual *suspects*

Apple
Pie

SERVES 6

Pastry

350 g/12 oz plain flour

pinch of salt

85 g/3 oz butter or margarine,
    cut into small pieces

85 g/3 oz lard or white vegetable fat,
    cut into small pieces

about 6 tbsp cold water

beaten egg or milk, for glazing

Filling

750 g–1 kg/1 lb 10 oz–2 lb 4 oz cooking
    apples, peeled, cored and sliced

125 g/4½ oz soft light brown or caster
    sugar, plus extra for sprinkling

½–1 tsp ground cinnamon, mixed
    spice or ground ginger

1–2 tbsp water (optional)

To make the pastry, sift the flour and salt into a mixing bowl. Add the butter and lard and rub them in with your fingertips until the mixture resembles fine breadcrumbs. Add the water and gather the mixture together into a dough. Wrap the dough in clingfilm and chill in the refrigerator for 30 minutes.

Preheat the oven to 220°C/425°F/Gas Mark 7. Roll out almost two thirds of the pastry thinly and use to line a deep 23-cm/9-inch pie dish.

To make the filling, mix the apples with the sugar and spice and pack into the pastry case; the filling can come up above the rim. Add the water, if needed, particularly if the apples are not very juicy.

Roll out the remaining pastry to form a lid. Dampen the edges of the pie rim with water and position the lid, pressing the edges firmly together. Trim and crimp the edges.

Use the trimmings to cut out leaves or other shapes to decorate the top of the pie. Dampen and attach. Glaze the top of the pie with beaten egg or milk, make 1 or 2 slits in the top and place the pie on a baking sheet.

Bake in the preheated oven for 20 minutes, then reduce the temperature to 180°C/350°F/Gas Mark 4 and bake for a further 30 minutes, or until the pastry is a light golden brown. Serve hot or cold, sprinkled with sugar.

Sticky
Toffee Pudding

SERVES 4

Pudding

75 g/2¾ oz sultanas

150 g/5½ oz stoned dates, chopped

1 tsp bicarbonate of soda

2 tbsp butter, plus extra for greasing

200 g/7 oz brown sugar

2 eggs

200 g/7 oz self-raising flour, sifted

Sticky Toffee Sauce

2 tbsp butter

175 ml/6 fl oz double cream

200 g/7 oz brown sugar

strips of orange zest, to decorate

To make the pudding, put the sultanas, dates and bicarbonate of soda into a heatproof bowl. Cover with boiling water and leave to soak.

Preheat the oven to 180°C/350°F/Gas Mark 4. Grease a 20-cm/8-inch round cake tin.

Put the butter in a separate bowl, add the sugar and mix well. Beat in the eggs, then fold in the flour. Drain the soaked fruits, add to the bowl and mix. Spoon the mixture evenly into the prepared cake tin. Transfer to the preheated oven and bake for 35–40 minutes. The pudding is cooked when a skewer inserted into the centre comes out clean.

About 5 minutes before the end of the cooking time, make the sauce. Melt the butter in a saucepan over a medium heat. Stir in the cream and sugar and bring to the boil, stirring constantly. Lower the heat and simmer for 5 minutes.

Turn out the pudding onto a serving plate and pour over the sauce. Decorate with orange zest and serve.

Black Forest
Gateau

SERVES 8

900 g/2 lb fresh cherries, stoned and
  halved

250 g/9 oz caster sugar

100 ml/3½ fl oz cherry brandy

100 g/3½ oz plain flour

50 g/1¾ oz cocoa powder

½ tsp baking powder

4 eggs

3 tbsp unsalted butter, melted, plus
  extra for greasing

1 litre/1¾ pints double cream

grated plain chocolate and whole
  fresh cherries, to decorate

Preheat the oven to 180°C/350°F/Gas Mark 4.
Grease and line a 23-cm/9-inch round springform
cake tin. Place the cherries in a saucepan, add
3 tablespoons of the sugar and the cherry brandy
and bring to a simmer over a medium heat.
Simmer for 5 minutes. Drain, reserving the syrup.

In a large bowl, sift together the flour, cocoa and baking powder. Place
the eggs in a heatproof bowl and beat in 160 g/5¾ oz of the sugar.
Place the bowl over a saucepan of simmering water and beat for
6 minutes, or until thickened. Remove from the heat, then gradually
fold in the flour mixture and the melted butter. Spoon into the cake
tin and bake in the preheated oven for 40 minutes. Remove from the
oven and leave to cool in the tin.

Turn out the cake and cut in half horizontally. Mix the double cream
and the remaining sugar together and whip lightly until soft peaks
form. Spread the reserved syrup over the cut sides of the cake, then
spread a layer of whipped cream on the bottom half of the cake,
followed by the cherries, and then place the other half on top. Cover
the top of the cake with whipped cream, sprinkle over the grated
chocolate and decorate with whole fresh cherries.

Treacle
Tart

SERVES 8

250 g/ 9 oz ready-made shortcrust
    pastry
plain flour, for dusting
350 g/12 oz golden syrup
125 g/4½ oz fresh white breadcrumbs
125 ml/4 fl oz double cream
finely grated rind of ½ lemon
    or orange
2 tbsp lemon juice or orange juice
whipped cream, to serve

Preheat the oven to 190°C/375°F/Gas Mark 5. Roll out the pastry on a lightly floured work surface and use to line a 20-cm/8-inch loose-based round tart tin, reserving the pastry trimmings. Prick the base of the pastry with a fork, cover with clingfilm and chill in the refrigerator.

Re-roll the pastry trimmings and stamp out small shapes, such as hearts, leaves or stars, to decorate the top of the tart.

Mix the golden syrup, breadcrumbs, double cream and lemon rind with the lemon juice in a small bowl. Pour the mixture into the pastry case and decorate the edges of the tart with the pastry cut-outs.

Transfer to the preheated oven and bake for 35–40 minutes, or until the filling is just set.

Leave the tart to cool slightly in the tin before turning out and serving with whipped cream.

Steamed Syrup
Sponge Pudding

SERVES 6

2 tbsp golden syrup, plus extra
  to serve
115 g/4 oz butter, plus extra
  for greasing
115 g/4 oz caster sugar
2 eggs, lightly beaten
175 g/6 oz self-raising flour
2 tbsp milk
grated rind of 1 lemon

Grease two 600-ml/1-pint pudding basins and put equal amounts of the syrup into the bottoms.

Beat together the butter and sugar until soft and creamy, then beat in the eggs, a little at a time.

Fold in the flour and stir in the milk to make a soft dropping consistency. Add the lemon rind. Divide the mixture between the two pudding basins.

Cover the surfaces with circles of greaseproof or baking paper and top with a pleated sheet of foil. Secure with some string or crimp the edges of the foil to ensure a tight fit around the basins.

Place the puddings in a large saucepan half-filled with boiling water. Cover the saucepan and bring back to the boil over a medium heat. Reduce the heat to a slow simmer and steam for 1½ hours, until risen and firm. Keep checking the water level and top up with boiling water as necessary.

Remove the pan from the heat and lift out the pudding basins. Remove the covers and loosen the puddings from the sides of the basins using a knife. Turn out onto a warmed serving plate and heat a little more syrup to serve with the puddings.

Rice
Pudding

SERVES 4–6

1 tbsp melted butter

115 g/4 oz pudding rice

55 g/2 oz caster sugar

850 ml/1½ pints full-cream milk

½ tsp vanilla extract

40 g/1½ oz unsalted butter

whole nutmeg, for grating

cream, jam, fruit purée, stewed fruit
  or ice cream, to serve (optional)

Preheat the oven to 150°C/300°F/Gas Mark 2. Grease a 1.2-litre/2-pint baking dish (a gratin dish is good) with the melted butter. Place the rice in the dish and sprinkle with the sugar.

Heat the milk in a saucepan until almost boiling, then pour over the rice. Add the vanilla extract and stir well to dissolve the sugar.

Cut the butter into small pieces and scatter over the surface of the pudding. Grate the whole nutmeg over the top, using as much as you like to give a good covering.

Place the dish on a baking tray and bake in the centre of the preheated oven for 1½–2 hours, until the pudding is well browned on the top. You can stir it after the first half hour to disperse the rice.

Serve hot with cream, jam, fruit purée, stewed fruit or ice cream, if desired.

Bread &
Butter Pudding

SERVES 4–6

85 g/3 oz butter, softened

6 thick slices of white bread

55 g/2 oz mixed dried fruit (sultanas,
   currants and raisins)

25 g/1 oz candied peel

3 large eggs

300 ml/10 fl oz milk

150 ml/5 fl oz double cream

55 g/2 oz caster sugar

whole nutmeg, for grating

1 tbsp demerara sugar

cream, to serve (optional)

Preheat the oven to 180°C/350°F/Gas Mark 4.
Use a little of the butter to grease a 20 x 25-cm/
8 x 10-inch baking dish, then spread the
remainder over the slices of bread. Cut
the bread into quarters and arrange half
overlapping in the dish.

Scatter half the dried fruit and peel over the bread, cover with the
remaining bread slices and add the remaining fruit and peel.

In a mixing jug, whisk the eggs well and mix in the milk, cream and
sugar. Pour this over the pudding and leave to stand for 15 minutes to
allow the bread to soak up some of the egg mixture. Tuck in most of
the fruit as you don't want it to burn in the oven. Grate the nutmeg
over the top of the pudding, according to taste, and sprinkle over the
demerara sugar.

Place the pudding on a baking tray and bake at the top of the
preheated oven for 30–40 minutes, until just set and golden brown.

Remove from the oven and serve warm with a little pouring cream,
if desired.

Rich Chocolate
Roulade

SERVES 4–6

Cake

butter, for greasing

125 g/4½ oz dark chocolate, chopped

50 g/1¾ oz Continental plain
   chocolate, chopped

3 tbsp warm water

2 tbsp coffee-flavoured liqueur, such
   as Kahlúa (optional)

5 eggs, separated

175 g/6 oz caster sugar

Filling

450 ml/16 fl oz double cream

40 g/1½ oz icing sugar, sifted, plus
   extra for dusting

20 g/¾ oz cocoa powder

2 tsp espresso coffee powder,
   dissolved in 1 tbsp boiling water

fresh raspberries, to serve

Preheat the oven to 180°C/350°F/Gas Mark 4.
Grease and line a 35 x 25-cm/14 x 10-inch Swiss
roll tin.

Put the chocolate into a heatproof bowl and
set over a saucepan of hot water, stirring
occasionally, until melted. Stir in the water and liqueur, if using. Whisk
the egg yolks and caster sugar in a bowl until pale. Beat the chocolate
into the egg yolk mixture. Whisk the egg whites in a clean bowl until
stiff, then fold into the chocolate mixture.

Pour into the prepared tin and bake in the preheated oven for
15 minutes. Remove, cover with greaseproof paper and leave to cool
for 3–4 hours. Meanwhile, whisk the filling ingredients together in a
bowl until thick. Cover with clingfilm and chill.

Turn the cake out onto greaseproof paper dusted with icing sugar.
Discard the lining paper. Spread the filling over the cake, leaving a
2.5-cm/1-inch border. Starting from a short side, roll up the cake.
Discard the paper. Serve immediately with fresh raspberries.

Banana
Splits

SERVES 4

4 bananas

6 tbsp chopped mixed nuts, to serve

Vanilla Ice Cream

300 ml/10 fl oz milk

1 tsp vanilla extract

3 egg yolks

100 g/3½ oz caster sugar

300 ml/10 fl oz double cream,
  whipped

Chocolate Rum Sauce

125 g/4½ oz plain chocolate, broken
  into small pieces

35 g/1¼ oz butter

6 tbsp water

1 tbsp rum

To make the ice cream, heat the milk and vanilla extract in a saucepan until almost boiling. In a bowl, beat together the egg yolks and sugar. Remove the milk from the heat and stir a little into the egg mixture. Transfer the mixture to the pan. Stir over a low heat until thick. Do not boil. Remove from the heat. Cool for 30 minutes, fold in the cream, cover with clingfilm and chill for 1 hour.

Transfer to an ice-cream maker and process for 15 minutes. Alternatively, transfer to a freezerproof container and freeze for 1 hour, then place in a bowl and beat to break up the ice crystals. Put back in the container and freeze for 30 minutes. Repeat twice more, freezing for 30 minutes and whisking each time.

To make the sauce, melt the chocolate and butter with the water in a saucepan, stirring. Remove from the heat and stir in the rum. Peel the bananas, slice lengthways and arrange on 4 serving dishes. Top with ice cream and nuts and serve with the sauce.

chocolate
galore

Chocolate
Fudge Cake

SERVES 8

175 g/6 oz butter, unsalted for preference, softened, plus extra for greasing

175 g/6 oz caster sugar

3 eggs, beaten

3 tbsp golden syrup

3 tbsp ground almonds

225 g/8 oz self-raising flour

pinch of salt

40 g/1½ oz cocoa powder

Icing

225 g/8 oz plain chocolate, broken into pieces

100 g/3½ oz dark muscovado sugar

225 g/8 oz butter, unsalted for preference, diced

5 tbsp evaporated milk

½ tsp vanilla extract

To make the icing, put the chocolate, sugar, butter, evaporated milk and vanilla extract in a heavy-based saucepan. Heat gently, stirring constantly, until melted. Pour into a bowl and leave to cool. Cover with clingfilm and leave to chill for 1 hour, or until spreadable.

Preheat the oven to 180°C/350°F/Gas Mark 4. Grease and line two 20-cm/8-inch sandwich tins.

To make the cake, put the butter and sugar in a bowl and beat until light and fluffy. Gradually beat in the eggs. Stir in the syrup and ground almonds. Sift the flour, salt and cocoa into a bowl, then fold into the mixture. Add a little water if necessary to make a dropping consistency. Spoon the mixture into the prepared tins and bake in the preheated oven for 30–35 minutes, until springy to the touch and a skewer inserted into the centre comes out clean.

Remove the cakes from the oven, leave in their tins for 5 minutes, then turn out onto wire racks to cool. When the cakes are completely cold, sandwich them together with half of the icing. Spread the remaining icing over the top and sides of the cake, swirling it to give a frosted appearance.

Chocolate
Fudge Brownies

MAKES 16

200 g/7 oz low-fat soft cheese

½ tsp vanilla extract

225 g/8 oz caster sugar

2 eggs

85 g/3 oz butter, plus extra
  for greasing

3 tbsp cocoa powder

100 g/3½ oz self-raising flour, sifted

50 g/1¾ oz pecan nuts, chopped

pecan nuts halves, to decorate
  (optional)

Fudge Icing

4 tbsp butter

1 tbsp milk

75 g/2¾ oz icing sugar

2 tbsp cocoa powder

Preheat the oven to 180°C/350°F/Gas Mark 4.
Lightly grease and line a 20-cm/8-inch square
shallow cake tin. Beat together the soft cheese,
vanilla extract and 5 teaspoons of the caster
sugar until smooth, then set aside.

Beat the eggs and the remaining caster sugar together until light
and fluffy. Place the butter and cocoa powder in a small pan and heat
gently, stirring until the butter melts and the mixture combines, then
stir it into the egg mixture. Fold in the flour and nuts.

Pour half of the cake mixture into the prepared tin and smooth
the top. Carefully spread the cheese mixture over it, then cover it
with the remaining cake mixture. Bake in the preheated oven for
40–45 minutes. Leave to cool in the pan.

To make the icing, melt the butter in a pan with the milk. Stir in the
icing sugar and cocoa powder. Spread the icing over the brownies and
decorate with pecan nut halves, if using. Let the icing set, then cut into
rectangles or squares to serve.

Double Chocolate Brownies
with Fudge Sauce

MAKES 9

115 g/4 oz butter, plus extra
  for greasing

115 g/4 oz plain chocolate, broken
  into pieces

300 g/10½ oz caster sugar

pinch of salt

1 tsp vanilla extract

2 large eggs

140 g/5 oz plain flour

2 tbsp cocoa powder

100 g/3½ oz white chocolate chips

Fudge Sauce

4 tbsp butter

225 g/8 oz golden caster sugar

150 ml/5 fl oz milk

250 ml/9 fl oz double cream

225 g/8 oz golden syrup

200 g/7 oz plain chocolate, broken
  into pieces

Preheat the oven to 180°C/350°F/Gas Mark 4. Grease and line an 18-cm/7-inch square cake tin. Place the butter and chocolate in a small heatproof bowl set over a saucepan of gently simmering water until melted. Stir until smooth. Leave to cool slightly. Stir in the sugar, salt and vanilla extract. Add the eggs, one at a time, and beat until blended.

Sift the flour and cocoa powder into the mixture and beat until smooth. Stir in the chocolate chips, then pour the mixture into the prepared tin. Bake in the preheated oven for 35–40 minutes, or until the top is evenly coloured and a fine skewer inserted into the centre comes out almost clean. Leave to cool slightly while you prepare the sauce.

To make the sauce, place the butter, sugar, milk, cream and syrup in a small saucepan and heat gently until the sugar has dissolved. Bring to the boil and stir for 10 minutes, or until the mixture is caramel-coloured. Remove from the heat and add the chocolate. Stir until smooth. Cut the brownies into squares and serve immediately with the sauce.

Mississippi
Mud Pie

SERVES 8

Pastry

225 g/8 oz plain flour, plus extra
   for dusting
2 tbsp cocoa powder
140 g/5 oz butter
2 tbsp caster sugar
1–2 tbsp cold water

Filling

175 g/6 oz butter
350 g/12 oz soft dark brown sugar
4 eggs, lightly beaten
4 tbsp cocoa powder, sifted
150 g/5½ oz plain chocolate, broken
   into pieces
300 ml/10 fl oz single cream
1 tsp chocolate extract
425 ml/15 fl oz double cream,
   whipped

chocolate flakes and curls,
   to decorate

To make the pastry, sift the flour and cocoa powder into a mixing bowl. Rub in the butter with your fingertips until the mixture resembles fine breadcrumbs. Stir in the sugar and enough cold water to mix to a soft dough. Wrap the dough in clingfilm and chill in the refrigerator for 15 minutes.

Preheat the oven to 190°C/375°F/Gas Mark 5. Roll out the pastry on a lightly floured work surface and use to line a 23-cm/9-inch loose-based tart tin. Line with greaseproof paper and fill with baking beans. Bake in the preheated oven for 15 minutes. Remove the paper and beans from the pastry case and cook for a further 10 minutes until crisp.

To make the filling, beat the butter and sugar together in a bowl and gradually beat in the eggs with the cocoa powder. Melt the chocolate and beat it into the mixture with the single cream and the chocolate extract.

Reduce the oven temperature to 160°C/325°F/Gas Mark 3. Pour the mixture into the pastry case and bake for 45 minutes, or until the filling has set gently. Let the mud pie cool completely, then transfer to a serving plate. Cover with the whipped cream. Decorate the pie with chocolate flakes and curls and then chill until ready to serve.

Rich Chocolate
Mousse

MAKES 4

300 g/10½ oz plain chocolate

5 tbsp caster sugar

20 g/¾ oz unsalted butter

1 tbsp brandy

4 eggs, separated

cocoa powder, for dusting

Break the chocolate into small pieces and put it in a heatproof bowl set over a saucepan of gently simmering water. Add the caster sugar and butter and melt together, stirring, until smooth. Remove from the heat, stir in the brandy, and leave to cool a little. Add the egg yolks and beat until smooth.

In a separate bowl, whisk the egg whites until stiff peaks form, then fold them into the chocolate mixture. Place a stainless steel cooking ring on each of 4 small serving plates, then spoon the mixture into each ring and smooth the surfaces. Transfer to the refrigerator and chill for at least 4 hours, until set.

Remove the mousses from the refrigerator and carefully remove the cooking rings. Dust with cocoa powder and serve immediately.

Chocolate
Éclairs

MAKES 12

Choux Pastry

150 ml/5 fl oz water

70 g/2½ oz butter, cut
  into small pieces, plus
  extra for greasing

100 g/3½ oz plain flour, sifted

2 eggs

Pastry Cream

2 eggs, lightly beaten

4 tbsp caster sugar

2 tbsp cornflour

300 ml/10 fl oz milk

¼ tsp vanilla extract

Topping

25 g/1 oz butter

1 tbsp milk

1 tbsp cocoa powder

55 g/2 oz icing sugar

50 g/1¾ oz white chocolate, melted

Preheat the oven to 200°C/400°F/Gas Mark 6. Lightly grease a baking sheet. Place the water in a saucepan, add the butter and heat gently until the butter melts. Bring to a rolling boil, then remove the saucepan from the heat and add the flour all at once, beating well until the mixture leaves the sides of the saucepan and forms a ball. Leave to cool slightly, then gradually beat in the eggs to form a smooth, glossy mixture. Spoon into a large piping bag fitted with a 1-cm/½-inch plain nozzle.

Sprinkle the baking sheet with a little water. Pipe éclairs 7.5 cm/3 inches long, spaced well apart. Bake in the preheated oven for 30–35 minutes, or until crisp and golden. Make a small slit in the side of each éclair to let the steam escape. Leave to cool on a wire rack.

Meanwhile, make the pastry cream. Whisk the eggs and sugar until thick and creamy, then fold in the cornflour. Heat the milk until almost boiling and pour onto the eggs, whisking. Transfer to the saucepan and cook over a low heat, stirring until thick. Remove the saucepan from the heat and stir in the vanilla extract. Cover with baking paper and leave to cool.

To make the icing, melt the butter with the milk in a saucepan, remove from the heat and stir in the cocoa and icing sugar. Split the éclairs lengthways and pipe in the pastry cream. Spread the icing over the top of the éclairs, then drizzle with the melted chocolate and leave to set.

Real
Hot Chocolate

SERVES 1–2

40 g/1½ oz plain chocolate, broken
  into pieces

300 ml/10 fl oz milk

chocolate curls, to decorate

Place the chocolate in a large heatproof jug. Place the milk in a heavy-based saucepan and bring to the boil. Pour about one quarter of the milk onto the chocolate and leave until the chocolate has softened.

Whisk the milk and chocolate mixture until smooth. Return the remaining milk to the heat and return to the boil, then pour onto the chocolate, whisking constantly.

Pour into warmed mugs or cups and decorate with chocolate curls. Serve immediately.

Chocolate
Fondue

SERVES 6

1 pineapple

1 mango

12 physalis

250 g/9 oz fresh strawberries

250 g/9 oz seedless white grapes

Fondue

250 g/9 oz plain chocolate, broken into pieces

150 ml/5 fl oz double cream

2 tbsp brandy

Using a sharp knife, peel and core the pineapple, then cut the flesh into cubes. Peel the mango and cut the flesh into cubes. Peel back the papery outer skin of the physalis and twist at the top to make a 'handle'. Arrange all the fruit on 6 serving plates and leave to chill in the refrigerator.

To make the fondue, place the chocolate and cream in a fondue pot. Heat gently, stirring constantly, until the chocolate has melted. Stir in the brandy until thoroughly blended and the chocolate mixture is smooth.

Place the fondue pot over the burner to keep warm. To serve, allow each guest to dip the fruit into the sauce, using fondue forks or bamboo skewers.

fruity favourites

Tarte
au Citron

SERVES 6–8

grated rind of 2–3 large lemons

150 ml/5 fl oz lemon juice

100 g/3½ oz caster sugar

125 ml/4 fl oz double cream or crème fraîche

3 large eggs

3 large egg yolks

icing sugar, for dusting

whole fresh raspberries, to serve

Pastry

175 g/6 oz plain flour, plus extra for dusting

½ tsp salt

115 g/4 oz cold unsalted butter, diced

1 egg yolk beaten with 2 tbsp ice-cold water

To make the pastry, sift the flour and salt into a large bowl. Add the butter and rub it in with your fingertips until the mixture resembles fine breadcrumbs. Add the egg yolk and water and stir to mix to a dough. Gather the dough into a ball, wrap in clingfilm and leave to chill in the refrigerator for at least 1 hour.

Preheat the oven to 200°C/400°F/Gas Mark 6. Roll the dough out on a lightly floured work surface and use to line a 23–25-cm/9–10-inch loose-based tart tin. Prick the base of the pastry case with a fork and line with baking paper and baking beans.

Bake in the preheated oven for 15 minutes, until the pastry looks set. Remove the paper and beans. Reduce the oven temperature to 190°C/375°F/Gas Mark 5.

Beat the lemon rind, lemon juice and sugar together until blended. Slowly beat in the cream, then beat in the eggs and yolks, one by one.

Set the pastry case on a baking sheet and pour in the filling. Transfer to the oven and bake for 20 minutes, until the filling is set. Leave to cool completely on a wire rack. Dust with icing sugar and serve with raspberries.

Apple & Blackberry
Crumble

SERVES 4

900 g/2 lb cooking apples, peeled
   and sliced
300 g/10½ oz blackberries, fresh
   or frozen
55 g/2 oz light muscovado sugar
1 tsp ground cinnamon
single or double cream,
   to serve

Crumble Topping

85 g/3 oz self-raising flour
85 g/3 oz plain wholemeal flour
115 g/4 oz unsalted butter
55 g/2 oz demerara sugar

Preheat the oven to 190°C/375°F/Gas Mark 5.

Peel and core the apples and cut into chunks.
Place in a bowl with the blackberries, muscovado
sugar and cinnamon and mix together, then
transfer to an ovenproof baking dish.

To make the crumble topping, sift the self-raising flour into a bowl
and stir in the wholemeal flour. Add the butter and rub in with your
fingers until the mixture resembles fine breadcrumbs. Stir in the
demerara sugar.

Spread the crumble over the fruit mixture and bake in the preheated
oven for 40–45 minutes, or until the apples are soft and the crumble is
golden brown and crisp.

Serve hot with cream.

Rhubarb
Crumble

SERVES 6

900 g/2 lb rhubarb

115 g/4 oz caster sugar

grated rind and juice of
 1 orange

cream, yogurt or custard,
 to serve

Crumble Topping

225 g/8 oz plain or
 wholemeal flour

115 g/4 oz unsalted butter

115 g/4 oz soft brown sugar

1 tsp ground ginger

Preheat the oven to 190°C/375°F/Gas Mark 5.

Cut the rhubarb into 2.5-cm/1-inch lengths and place in a 1.7-litre/3-pint ovenproof dish with the sugar and the orange rind and juice.

To make the crumble topping, place the flour in a mixing bowl and rub in the butter with your fingertips until the mixture resembles breadcrumbs. Stir in the sugar and ginger.

Spread the crumble evenly over the fruit and press down lightly using a fork. Bake in the centre of the preheated oven on a baking tray for 25–30 minutes, until the crumble is golden brown.

Serve warm with cream, yogurt or custard.

Fruit
Cobbler

SERVES 6

900 g/2 lb fresh berries and currants,
   such as blackberries, blueberries,
   raspberries, redcurrants and
   blackcurrants
85–115 g/3–4 oz caster sugar
2 tbsp cornflour
single or double cream, to serve

Cobbler Topping

200 g/7 oz plain flour
2 tsp baking powder
pinch of salt
55 g/2 oz unsalted butter, diced
   and chilled
2 tbsp caster sugar
175 ml/6 fl oz buttermilk
1 tbsp demerara sugar

Preheat the oven to 200°C/400°F/Gas Mark 6.

Pick over the fruit, mix with the sugar and cornflour and put in a 25-cm/10-inch shallow ovenproof dish.

To make the cobbler topping, sift the flour, baking powder and salt into a large bowl. Rub in the butter with your fingertips until the mixture resembles breadcrumbs, then stir in the sugar. Pour in the buttermilk and mix to a soft dough.

Drop spoonfuls of the dough on top of the fruit roughly, so that it doesn't completely cover the fruit. Sprinkle with the demerara sugar and bake in the preheated oven for 25–30 minutes, until the crust is golden and the fruit is tender.

Remove from the oven and leave to stand for a few minutes before serving with cream.

Latticed
Cherry Pie

SERVES 8

Pastry

140 g/5 oz plain flour, plus extra for dusting

¼ tsp baking powder

½ tsp mixed spice

½ tsp salt

50 g/1¾ oz caster sugar

55 g/2 oz cold unsalted butter, diced, plus extra for greasing

1 egg, beaten, plus extra for glazing

Filling

900 g/2 lb stoned fresh cherries, or canned cherries, drained

150 g/5 oz caster sugar

½ tsp almond extract

2 tsp cherry brandy

¼ tsp mixed spice

2 tbsp cornflour

2 tbsp water

25 g/1 oz unsalted butter

To make the pastry, sift the flour with the baking powder into a large bowl. Stir in the mixed spice, salt and sugar. Using your fingertips, rub in the butter until the mixture resembles fine breadcrumbs, then pour in the beaten egg and mix to a dough. Cut the dough in half and roll each half into a ball. Wrap the dough in clingfilm and chill in the refrigerator for 30 minutes.

Preheat the oven to 220°C/425°F/Gas Mark 7. Grease a 23-cm/9-inch round pie dish with butter. Roll out the pastry into 2 rounds, each 30 cm/12 inches in diameter. Use one to line the pie dish. Trim the edges, leaving an overhang of 1 cm/½ inch.

To make the filling, put half of the cherries and the sugar in a large saucepan. Bring to a simmer over a low heat, stirring, and cook for 5 minutes, or until the sugar has melted. Stir in the almond extract, brandy and mixed spice. In a separate bowl, mix the cornflour and water to form a paste. Remove the saucepan from the heat, stir in the cornflour paste, then return to the heat and stir constantly until the mixture boils and thickens. Leave to cool a little. Stir in the remaining cherries, pour into the pastry case, then dot with butter.

Cut the remaining pastry round into long strips 1 cm/½ inch wide. Lay the strips evenly on the top of the filling, criss-crossing to form a lattice. Trim off the ends and seal the edges with water. Use your fingers to crimp around the rim, then brush the top with beaten egg. Cover with kitchen foil, then bake in the preheated oven for 30 minutes. Discard the foil, then bake the pie for a further 15 minutes, or until cooked and golden. Serve warm.

Pumpkin
Pie

SERVES 6

1.8 kg/4 lb sweet pumpkin

140 g/5 oz plain flour, plus extra
  for dusting

¼ tsp baking powder

1½ tsp ground cinnamon

¾ tsp ground nutmeg

¾ tsp ground cloves

1 tsp salt

50 g/1¾ oz caster sugar

55 g/2 oz cold unsalted butter, diced,
  plus extra for greasing

3 eggs

400 ml/14 fl oz canned sweetened
  condensed milk

½ tsp vanilla extract

1 tbsp demerara sugar

Streusel Topping

2 tbsp plain flour

4 tbsp demerara sugar

1 tsp ground cinnamon

2 tbsp cold unsalted butter, cut into
  small pieces

75 g/2¾ oz pecan nuts, chopped

75 g/2¾ oz walnuts, chopped

Preheat the oven to 190°C/375°F/Gas Mark 5. Halve the pumpkin. Remove and discard the seeds, stem and stringy insides. Put the pumpkin halves, face down, in a shallow baking tin and cover with foil. Bake in the preheated oven for 1½ hours then leave to cool. Scoop out the flesh, mash in a large bowl, and drain away any excess liquid. Cover and chill until ready to use.

Grease a 23-cm/9-inch round pie dish. Sift the flour and baking powder into a large bowl. Stir in ½ tsp cinnamon, ¼ tsp nutmeg, ¼ tsp cloves, ½ tsp salt and all the caster sugar. Rub in the butter with your fingertips until the mixture resembles fine breadcrumbs. Lightly beat 1 egg and pour it into the bowl. Mix together to a soft dough. Roll out the pastry on a lightly floured surface and use to line the pie dish, trimming the edges. Cover and chill in the refrigerator for 30 minutes.

Preheat the oven to 220°C/425°F/Gas Mark 7. Stir the condensed milk and remaining eggs into the pumpkin purée. Add the remaining spices and salt, then stir in the vanilla extract and sugar. Pour into the pastry case and bake in the preheated oven for 15 minutes.

Meanwhile, combine the flour, sugar and cinnamon in a bowl, rub in the butter until crumbly, then stir in the nuts. Remove the pie from the oven and reduce the heat to 180°C/350°F/Gas Mark 4. Sprinkle the topping over the pie, then bake for a further 35 minutes. Serve hot or cold.

Blueberry
Clafoutis

SERVES 4

2 tbsp butter, plus extra for greasing

125 g/4½ oz caster sugar

3 eggs

60 g/2¼ oz plain flour

250 ml/9 fl oz single cream, plus
  extra to serve

½ tsp ground cinnamon

450 g/1 lb blueberries

icing sugar, for dusting

Preheat the oven to 180°C/350°F/Gas Mark 4.
Grease a 1-litre/1¾-pint ovenproof dish.

Put the butter in a bowl with the sugar and
whisk together until fluffy. Add the eggs and
beat together well. Mix in the flour, then
gradually stir in the cream followed by the cinnamon. Continue to stir
until smooth.

Arrange the blueberries in the base of the prepared dish, then pour
over the cream batter. Transfer to the preheated oven and bake for
about 30 minutes, or until puffed and golden.

Remove from the oven, dust lightly with icing sugar and serve with
single cream.

Chocolate
Blueberry Pies

MAKES 10

Pastry

175 g/6 oz plain flour

40 g/1½ oz cocoa powder

55 g/2 oz caster sugar

pinch of salt

125 g/4½ oz butter, cut into small
  pieces

1 egg yolk

1–2 tbsp cold water

Blueberry Topping

200 g/7 oz blueberries

2 tbsp crème de cassis

10 g/¼ oz icing sugar, sifted

Chocolate Filling

140 g/5 oz plain chocolate

225 ml/8 fl oz double cream

150 ml/5 fl oz soured cream or crème
  fraîche

To make the pastry, put the flour, cocoa, sugar and salt in a large
bowl and rub in the butter with your fingertips until the mixture
resembles breadcrumbs. Add the egg yolk and a little cold water to
form a dough. Wrap the dough in clingfilm and chill in the refrigerator
for 30 minutes.

Remove the dough from the refrigerator and roll out. Use to line
ten 10-cm/4-inch tartlet tins. Freeze for 30 minutes. Preheat the
oven to 180°C/350°F/Gas Mark 4. Bake the tartlets in the preheated
oven for 15–20 minutes. Leave to cool.

Put the blueberries, cassis and icing sugar in a saucepan and warm
through so that the berries become shiny but do not burst. Leave
to cool.

To make the filling, melt the chocolate in a heatproof bowl set over
a pan of gently simmering water, then cool slightly. Whip the cream
until stiff and fold in the soured cream and melted chocolate.

Transfer the tartlet cases to a serving plate and divide the chocolate
filling among them, smoothing the surface with a palette knife, then
top with the blueberries.

cool
classics

Rich Vanilla
Ice Cream

SERVES 4–6

300 ml/10 fl oz single cream and
   300 ml/10 fl oz double cream or
   600 ml/1 pint whipping cream
1 vanilla pod
4 large egg yolks
115 g/4 oz caster sugar

Pour the single and double cream or the whipping cream into a large heavy-based saucepan. Split open the vanilla pod and scrape out the seeds into the cream, then add the whole vanilla pod too. Bring almost to the boil, then remove from the heat and leave to infuse for 30 minutes.

Put the egg yolks and sugar in a large bowl and whisk together until pale and the mixture leaves a trail when the whisk is lifted. Remove the vanilla pod from the cream, then slowly add the cream to the egg mixture, stirring all the time with a wooden spoon. Strain the mixture into the rinsed-out saucepan or a double boiler and cook over a low heat for 10–15 minutes, stirring all the time, until the mixture thickens enough to coat the back of the spoon. Do not allow the mixture to boil or it will curdle. Remove the custard from the heat and leave to cool for at least 1 hour, stirring from time to time to prevent a skin from forming.

If using an ice cream machine, churn the cold custard in the machine following the manufacturer's instructions. Alternatively, freeze the custard in a freezerproof container, uncovered, for 1–2 hours, or until it begins to set around the edges. Turn the custard into a bowl and stir with a fork or beat in a food processor until smooth. Return to the freezer and freeze for a further 2–3 hours, or until firm. Cover the container with a lid for storing.

Trifle

SERVES 4

Fruit Layer

6 trifle sponge cakes

2 tbsp strawberry jam

6 large strawberries, hulled and
   sliced

2 bananas, peeled and sliced

400 g/14 oz canned sliced peaches,
   drained

6 tbsp sherry

Custard Layer

250 ml/9 fl oz double cream

1 tsp vanilla extract

3 egg yolks

4 tbsp caster sugar

Topping

300 ml/10 fl oz double cream

2 tbsp caster sugar

1 tbsp chopped mixed nuts, toasted

strawberry halves, to decorate

To make the fruit layer, spread the sponge cakes with jam, cut into bite-sized pieces and arrange in the base of a glass serving bowl. Scatter over the fruit, pour over the sherry and set aside.

To make the custard, place the cream and vanilla extract in a saucepan and bring almost to the boil over a low heat. Meanwhile, place the egg yolks and sugar in a pudding basin and whisk together. Remove the cream mixture from the heat and gradually stir into the egg mixture. Return the mixture to the saucepan and warm over a low heat, stirring, until thickened. Remove the custard from the heat and leave to cool for 30 minutes, then pour it over the fruit layer. Cover with clingfilm and chill for 2½ hours.

Remove the trifle from the refrigerator. To make the topping, whip the cream and sugar together, then spread it evenly over the custard layer. Scatter the chopped nuts over the top, then cover again with clingfilm and chill for a further 1½ hours. Serve decorated with strawberry halves.

Crème
Caramel

SERVES 4–6

butter, for greasing

175 g/6 oz plus 2 tbsp caster sugar

4 tbsp water

½ lemon

500 ml/18 fl oz milk

1 vanilla pod

2 large eggs

2 large egg yolks

fresh mint leaves, to decorate

Preheat the oven to 160°C/325°F/Gas Mark 3. Lightly grease the base and sides of two 600-ml/1-pint soufflé dishes. To make the caramel, place 75 g/2¾ oz of the sugar with the water in a saucepan over a medium–high heat and cook, stirring, until the sugar dissolves. Boil until the syrup turns a deep golden brown. Immediately remove from the heat and squeeze in a few drops of lemon juice. Divide evenly between the soufflé dishes and swirl around. Set aside.

Pour the milk into a saucepan. Slit the vanilla pod lengthways and add it to the milk. Bring to the boil, remove the saucepan from the heat and stir in the remaining sugar, stirring until it dissolves. Reserve.

Beat the eggs and egg yolks together in a bowl. Pour the milk mixture over them, whisking. Remove the vanilla pod. Strain the egg mixture into a bowl, then divide evenly between the soufflé dishes.

Place the dishes in a roasting tin with enough boiling water to come two thirds up the sides. Bake in the preheated oven for 1–1¼ hours, or until a knife inserted in the centre comes out clean. Leave to cool completely. Cover and leave to chill for at least 24 hours.

Run a round-bladed knife around the edge of each dish. Invert the soufflé dishes onto a serving plate. Lift off the dishes and serve decorated with mint leaves.

Tiramisù

SERVES 4

200 ml/7 fl oz strong black coffee,
  cooled to room temperature
4 tbsp orange liqueur,
  such as Cointreau
3 tbsp orange juice
16 Italian sponge fingers
250 g/9 oz mascarpone cheese
300 ml/10 fl oz double cream, lightly
  whipped
3 tbsp icing sugar
grated rind of 1 orange

To Decorate

chopped toasted almonds
strips of lemon zest
chocolate shavings

Pour the cooled coffee into a jug and stir in the orange liqueur and orange juice. Put 8 of the sponge fingers in the bottom of a serving dish, then pour over half of the coffee mixture.

Place the mascarpone cheese in a bowl with the cream, icing sugar and orange rind and mix together well. Spread half of the mascarpone mixture over the coffee-soaked sponge fingers, then arrange the remaining sponge fingers on top. Pour over the remaining coffee mixture and then spread over the remaining mascarpone mixture. Chill in the refrigerator for at least 2 hours.

Serve decorated with chopped toasted almonds, strips of lemon zest and chocolate shavings.

Profiteroles
with Chocolate Sauce

SERVES 4

Choux Pastry

200 ml/7 fl oz water

70 g/2½ oz butter, plus extra
   for greasing

100 g/3½ oz plain flour

3 eggs, beaten

Cream Filling

300 ml/10 fl oz double cream

3 tbsp caster sugar

1 tsp vanilla extract

Chocolate Sauce

125 g/4½ oz plain chocolate, broken
   into small pieces

35 g/1¼ oz butter

6 tbsp water

2 tbsp brandy

Preheat the oven to 200°C/400°F/Gas Mark 6. Grease a large baking tray. To make the pastry, put the water and butter into a saucepan and bring to the boil. Meanwhile, sift the flour into a bowl. Immediately add all the flour, remove the pan from the heat and stir the mixture into a paste that leaves the sides of the saucepan clean. Leave to cool slightly. Beat in enough of the eggs to give the mixture a soft, dropping consistency.

Transfer to a piping bag fitted with a 1-cm/½-inch plain nozzle. Pipe small balls onto the baking tray. Bake in the preheated oven for 25 minutes. Remove from the oven. Pierce each ball with a skewer to let the steam escape.

To make the filling, whip together the cream, sugar and vanilla extract. Cut the pastry balls almost in half, then fill with cream.

To make the sauce, melt the chocolate and butter with the water in a heatproof bowl set over a saucepan of gently simmering water, stirring until smooth. Stir in the brandy. Pile the profiteroles into individual serving dishes or into a pyramid on a raised cake stand. Pour over the sauce and serve.

Strawberry
Cheesecake

SERVES 8

Base

55 g/2 oz butter, preferably unsalted

200 g/7 oz digestive biscuits, crushed

85 g/3 oz chopped walnuts

Filling

450 g/1 lb mascarpone cheese

2 eggs, beaten

3 tbsp caster sugar

250 g/9 oz white chocolate, broken
  into pieces

300 g/10½ oz strawberries, hulled
  and quartered

Topping

175 g/6 oz mascarpone cheese

50 g/1¾ oz white chocolate shavings

4 strawberries, halved

Preheat the oven to 150°C/300°F/Gas Mark 2. Melt the butter in a saucepan over a low heat and stir in the crushed biscuits and nuts. Spoon into a 23-cm/9-inch round springform cake tin and press evenly over the base with the back of a spoon. Set aside.

To make the filling, beat the mascarpone cheese in a bowl until smooth, then beat in the eggs and sugar. Melt the white chocolate in a heatproof bowl set over a saucepan of gently simmering water, stirring until smooth. Remove from the heat and leave to cool slightly, then stir into the cheese mixture. Stir in the strawberries.

Spoon the mixture into the cake tin, spread out evenly and smooth the surface. Bake in the preheated oven for 1 hour, or until the filling is just firm. Turn off the oven and leave the cheesecake to cool inside with the door slightly ajar until completely cold. Transfer to a serving plate.

For the topping, spread the mascarpone cheese on top. Decorate with the chocolate shavings and the strawberry halves.

Blueberry
Cheesecake

SERVES 8–10

sunflower oil, for brushing

85 g/3 oz butter

200 g/7 oz digestive biscuits, crushed

400 g/14 oz cream cheese

2 large eggs

140 g/5 oz caster sugar

1½ tsp vanilla extract

450 ml/16 fl oz soured cream

Blueberry Topping

55 g/2 oz caster sugar

4 tbsp water

250 g/9 oz fresh blueberries

1 tsp arrowroot

Preheat the oven to 190°C/375°F/Gas Mark 5. Brush a 20-cm/8-inch round springform tin with oil. Melt the butter in a saucepan over a low heat. Stir in the biscuits, then spread in the tin. Place the cream cheese, eggs, 100 g/3½ oz of the sugar and ½ teaspoon of the vanilla extract in a food processor. Process until smooth. Pour over the biscuit base and smooth the top. Place on a baking tray and bake in the preheated oven for 20 minutes, until set. Remove from the oven and leave for 20 minutes. Leave the oven switched on.

Mix the soured cream with the remaining sugar and vanilla extract in a bowl. Spoon over the cheesecake. Return it to the oven for 10 minutes, leave to cool, then cover with clingfilm and chill in the refrigerator for 8 hours, or overnight.

To make the topping, place the sugar in a saucepan with 2 tablespoons of the water over a low heat and stir until the sugar has dissolved. Increase the heat, add the blueberries, cover and cook for a few minutes, or until they begin to soften. Remove from the heat. Mix the arrowroot and remaining water in a bowl, add to the pan and stir until smooth. Return to a low heat. Cook until the juice thickens and turns translucent. Leave to cool. Remove the cheesecake from the tin 1 hour before serving. Spoon over the blueberry topping and chill until ready to serve.

Summer
Pudding

SERVES 6

900 g/2 lb mixed berries, such
   as blackberries, blueberries,
   raspberries and strawberries
140 g/5 oz caster sugar
125 ml/4 fl oz milk
8 slices day-old white bread, crusts
   removed

Hull the berries and put them in a bowl. Sprinkle with the sugar and set aside.

Sprinkle the milk over the slices of bread to soften them slightly. Line the base and sides of a pudding basin with two thirds of the bread, cutting it to fit but overlapping the edges slightly. Spoon the berries into the basin and place the remaining bread slices on top, cutting to fit and making sure that the fruit is completely covered.

Place a round of greaseproof paper on top of the last layer of bread. Put a plate or saucer, slightly smaller than the diameter of the basin, on top, then place a weight, such as a heavy can of fruit, on the plate. Leave to chill in the refrigerator for at least 8 hours.

To serve, remove the weight, plate and greaseproof paper. Invert a serving dish on top of the basin and, holding them together, reverse and shake sharply – the pudding should slide out. Serve immediately.